CHOSEN

A Book About – You

WAYNE SUTTON

Table of Contents

Introduction 3
The Wide-eyed Teenage Entrepreneurs 7
The Power of Two Words 16
Hope 17
My Dad 20
Your Experiences Are Seeds 26
Opportunity 29
Mentor 34
Sifting 38
Why Sifting and Sorting? 46

Introduction

This book is about one simple thing – you.

Yep, you.

Look around, even now as you are reading this.

Yeah. It's you.

If you've ever read a book, heard a speech or had a moment that changed your life... welcome back.

This is your calling, that magical moment awakening you again from the slumber of mundane life... knowing there is more.

Yes – You!

Read this book because it was written for you or pass it on if you are scared to admit there is more for your life.

This book is about money.

This book is about your calling and purpose.

This book is about business.

And, this book is about life.

Your life.

They are the same you know.

This book not only holds the power to create wealth in your life, but it can also awaken your purpose.

Finally

Bold statement?

Yes.

Yet, you are still reading for a number of reasons.

Why?

What's your reason?

Your dreams?

This book is a gift to you from the person who gave it to you.

You didn't buy this book.

Someone bought it for you.

Why?

That person believes in you.

That person chose you.

Now, choose yourself.

And enjoy this gift....

Have you ever read a book that did more than just catch your attention, but it actually shifted the way you thought about something?

Have you ever read a book, heard a speech or been fortunate enough to meet someone who truly changed your life?

Have you ever picked up a book and found that you could not dare set it down until you had absorbed every single morsel of truth?

Or maybe you can think back to a time when you bought a book that impacted your heart and life so much, you had to buy more and more copies to give away to others.

This book may very well give you that type of experience or it may not.

Most importantly, I invite you to notice how it makes you think – the ideas, feelings, and emotions it generates.

Open your mind to what this short book can do for you.

Wayne Sutton

The Wide-eyed Teenage Entrepreneurs

As I said earlier, this book is about money, life, and you. So, I will start with a quick story about myself.

See, when I was 13 years old, I began my life as an "entrepreneur."

And even though I failed miserably, the experiences I learned from it created vast amounts of success for me over the last few decades.

I worked about 20 hours a week at a local grocery store bagging groceries, stocking shelves, and mopping the floors.

I had no clue about the real world of work, but I was happy to put on my apron and go to work with the older teenagers and adults.

My older cousin, who happened to be 16 years old, was doing some light carpentry work at the apartment complex just behind the grocery store.

One evening, he drove up to give me a ride home and muttered excitedly, "Look! I have found something. We're going to be rich!"

Now, for a 13-year-old, I thought, "Hey, that sounds good, and it's definitely possible because my older cousin said so."

The logic of teenagers, huh. :-)

He showed me a program he had purchased on how to get rich in mail order, and how we would become absolutely wealthy by just placing classified ads in newspapers.

Getting rich by placing small classified ads to reach a few thousand people sounded easy enough. But, we thought if newspapers could reach thousands, why not get the attention of hundreds of thousands by placing our ad in a supermarket tabloid?

So, we worked. I bagged the groceries and my cousin lifted plywood and cleaned up loose nails. We put our money together to buy one single ad in the *National Enquirer*.

Yep, the grocery store tabloid was going to build us a financial legacy!

We rushed and rented a post office box. We had an information product printed for order fulfillment. And just like that, at 13 years old, I was a proud partner of an international mail order company.

Hey, it sounded good. :-)

Next, we researched and found a way to have an informational voicemail set up. We actually paid a voice-over actor to make the recording for the voicemail. And finally, we scraped up the money to have a classified ad placed in one single issue of the *National Enquirer*.

So, we invested about $350 in the *National Enquirer* ad, about $50 in the post office box, and another $100 or so for a voice-over actor to record our voicemail.

That was about $500 of hard earned money all in, and the ad came out. In fact, we were about 502 bucks into this endeavor because we had to pick up our proof copy of the *National Enquirer*.

This was going to make us rich, right?

We looked at the ad over and over and then we rushed to the post office...every... single... day. Every day.

Every day, we would drive to the post office and wait for our riches. We would slide the key, turn it, open up the door, but we saw nothing except an empty box. And so we continued.

We went back the next day... and the next day... and the next day. After nine days we had lost hope.

We were tired of opening an empty post office box all the time.

We had no problem collecting pizza coupons and sales flyer, but we never saw a single order from our endeavor.

Until.

Ten days later, I took the keys from my cousin, bent down to open Box 272 and as we opened it up we witnessed magic happen!

I remember sliding the key into the lock, turning it to the right, pulling it open, and there was an envelope.

There was one single envelope from Buffalo, New York!

We quickly ripped it open, and I can still see in my mind the money order made out to the name of our company, which I have long forgotten.

It was $16.95 to purchase our product! But we could not even cash the money order because we were 13 and 16- year-old kids without a bank account!

However, we sent the person the product we had promised, and at that moment, we felt beyond successful!

Yes, we lost money, but we came to realize that if we could bring the message the people wanted, they would respond with orders for our products, and we could earn an income!

We were true entrepreneurs, *even if we had failed miserably.*

The point of this story is really simple. If you bring value to people, they will reward you financially.

At the time our entrepreneurial venture failed, we were 13 and 16 years old. However, many people today fail regardless of their ages or backgrounds when it comes to being entrepreneurs.

What I realized at 13 years old and today in my forties is that many people want to break out of this mindset of feeling stuck.

Many feel stuck in their relationships, careers, finances, and life in general.

Some people don't know where they want to go, while others don't know how to get where they want to go. It is an uncomfortable and troubling position to be in.

As you're reading this book, thinking about the silly story I have just told, and about your journey, do you feel stuck?

Do you have that feeling where you know there's something more for you?

Do you know there's a purpose and a passion for you to follow, but you've never been able to walk into that reality?

Is there no one to help you along the journey?

Does this sound familiar to you?

Is this starting to conjure up a thought within you, maybe an emotional response?

Have you said to yourself, "That's right"?

This book will take you on a journey that will awaken that hidden, maybe even buried purpose and help you make it a reality.

The person who gave you this book did so because he or she saw something within you, something special – a character trait or a hint of your personality that has great potential.

Sometimes people can see things about us that we don't even see ourselves!

If you're like me, you're probably saying, "That's right. There's something more for me."

In the next few pages, we're going to give you the opportunity to see if you can once again awaken to that purpose.

Can a book change your life?

Can a moment in time truly enhance your future?

I believe so!

Enjoy the journey...

The Power of Two Words

Instead of telling you another story of my days as a teenage entrepreneur, I want to share with you the power of 2 words that I believe the world itself is lacking today.

The first word is hope.

Hope

When you hear the word "hope," what thoughts do you have? What images seem to pop up in the front of your mind?

Sadly, most people only know the word "hope" as a magical wish or prayer against some major fear they are letting rule their lives.

"I hope I don't lose my job."

"I hope my spouse loves me."

"I hope my car lasts me another year or two."

Do any of these sound familiar? Have you unconsciously blurted out any of these yourself? I surely have.

The word "hope" should actually be a word of expectancy, not one spoken in fear or doubt. When we speak it in doubt, we lose the divine power of the word.

One of my favorite passages about Hope comes from the Bible: "And now these three remain: faith, hope and love". (1 Corinthians 13:13).

So, what does the word "hope" really mean, and why is that important to you?

I went to the good ol' Google for a definition and here is what I found on Wikipedia:

> Hope is an optimistic state of mind that is based on an expectation of positive outcomes with respect to events and circumstances in one's life or the world at large. As a verb, its definitions include: "expect with confidence" and "to cherish a desire with anticipation."

That sounds a lot different from the same ol' "I hope my car doesn't break down, and I hope my spouse loves me." Wouldn't you agree?

"Expect with confidence." With confidence means positivity and, in my mind, at least, happiness! Not fear or doubt.

"To cherish a desire with anticipation." Again, do you hear any fear or doubt in that statement?

At the age of 13, I had a desire to build wealth in partnership with my cousin.

I had not been programmed by the world that it was impossible to do with a single ad in a tabloid.

I wanted the money, but the desire was much deeper than $100 bills and a fancy money clip.

My Dad

Have you ever had someone in your life you wanted to just bless and give back to?

Is there someone you want to not only make proud but also to help financially?

My mother passed away when I was seven years old, and I witnessed my dad battle her loss for the remainder of his life, both in his heart and in his finances.

The first thing my dad did when he learned about my teenage entrepreneurial endeavors was to laugh.

Then, trying to save me from failure and disappointment, he sorrowfully told me, "Son, you were born poor, and you will die poor."

Wow.

Over 30 years later, I can still see my dad trying to save his son from his crazy dreams. The "born poor" was definitely true.

However, the "You will die poor" omen from my dad was a choice for me to agree or disagree with and create my own life. My dad may have given me bad advice, but he meant well.

Has someone you truly love ever given you "bad advice" in your life?

Is there someone you care about who does not believe in you or your dreams?

Yep.

You still love them, right?

That's OK.

You can love someone but still not let them direct your dreams and your life!

Think about the times in your life that very well-meaning people have spoken limited beliefs and imposed their doubts and fears on you.

Has anyone ever told you to "be realistic"?

This kills dreams and goals that have potential!

Can you imagine someone telling Henry Ford that a horseless carriage built in mass would never work, and he needed to "be realistic"?

What about Steve Jobs?

Ever heard about the iPad? Are you using an iPhone?

What if he was simply "realistic"?

Oh, here is another one: has anyone ever told you to "Be careful"?

Be careful?

That makes sense when you are driving on the freeway at 80 miles per hour, but not when you are trying to break out of the mold of an average income.

Always remember – mediocrity loves carefulness and fear-based actions.

Do you?

Nope.

If you're still reading this book, I'm sure you are already recognizing that you are different and ready to see where this is leading.

You were created with a hope and calling for greatness within you!

Regardless of what has happened in your life up until this point, I believe the passion and purpose are still within you crying out to be released!

I failed at 13.

Again at 15.

And 18. Then 23. Then 27.

And again…

I failed many times. Yet, I decided that every failure was a lesson in life and a lesson in learning about the REAL ME!

Have you ever failed?

I invite you to consider the experience for a moment.

I want you to see, not the moment of failure but instead, what you gained from the experience and the knowledge you acquired from that event.

I truly believe there is no longer failure in my life – only feedback.

Failure implies that it's over.

Feedback implies that regardless of the current situation, I am learning and readjusting.

Therefore, I will succeed!

I invite you to consider the same.

All the things in your past that looked like failures: relationships, career choices, business opportunities, and so forth, whatever you thought you "failed" at in that season of life, I urge you to reconsider as places of learning and feedback!

Still with me?

Your Experiences Are Seeds

You have not failed!

You took something away from what you went through – experience. Your "failure" gave you a lesson called experience.

Your experiences are seeds that sprout forth as future decisions.

Your seeds of experience sprout in your future decisions based on your viewpoint or your mindset.

If you look at an experience or set of experiences with a mindset of gratitude for the lesson, you will sprout forth actions based on a foundation of expectation and positivity.

Likewise, if you view the same experience or experiences with a mindset of failure and defeat then – you guessed it – your actions will sprout forth negativity and most likely, poor results.

You have no failure.

You only have feedback!

Say it with me, "I have no failure. I only have feedback!"

When you have feedback, you can create change and truly design or redesign your life! Your mindset is a powerful key to your victory and breakthrough.

That's exciting because your mindset is yours to change at any time!

Still reading?

You just may be one of the chosen.

How do you know? Ask yourself what parts of the above content have already resonated with you?

What areas above have made you say, *"that's right"*?

The first word I shared with you is hope. The second word I will share that can change your life now is the word "opportunity."

Opportunity

What does that word "opportunity" mean to you?

What emotions rise up within you when you hear that word?

There are really two "thoughts" that come up when someone hears the word "opportunity." Both thoughts tell a lot about the "opportunities" that person will have available in his or her life.

The first thought is based on excitement!

Do you know that feeling you have when you see or hear something that causes you to feel instantly excited and ready to discover even more?

Can you think back to a time when you were truly curious and even excited at the same time?

How does reflecting on those times feel now?

I ask you to truly relish those feelings for a moment to discover more, and ask yourself when was the last time you felt that way.

Again, you are reading this book for a reason.

Chosen.

Someone chose you to read this book, and I am sure you have already felt that calling to choose yourself for a change as well.

I understand.

I get ya' because I too have felt the calling within, not only the calling for me to accomplish, but to live my life fully!

And the calling is often an inner scream.

So, why were you chosen, and what does it mean for you?

The only difference between a 13-year old entrepreneur and one at your current age is the opportunities that exist today.

We live in an amazing time for entrepreneurship, one unlike any other.

It can be your path to accomplish all you have dreamed about for so long.

In the past 100 or so years, the world has witnessed revolutionary inventions and technological advancements in automobiles, airplanes, and other innovations.

We have even seen man's exploration of the outer space. More recently, the internet and cell phones have changed our world and the way we communicate in ways never imagined.

We live in an absolutely amazing time of history.

Literally, the world's information can now fit in the palm of your hand!

In the last 3 years, I've interviewed teenagers who are self-made millionaires, as well as stay-at-home moms earning more money than their husbands who are working at the office 60 hours per week!

Are you ready for more?

Would you object to a true opportunity to not only awaken the hope within you but also make your hidden dreams a reality?

Of course, you wouldn't!

That's why you're still reading.

So what do a stay-at-home mom and a pimple-faced millionaire teenager have in common? Why are they both more successful than 98% of the daily grinding workforce?

You're about to have a profound realization.

One simple word.

Ready for it?

Here ya go...

The truly successful person has one thing that most other people simply don't...

Mentor

That's the obvious key to success.

So, at age 13, I failed as an entrepreneur. Yet, today, I not only succeed but also help others from all over the world prosper.

I met a mentor.

Someone handed me a book very similar to this book you are reading now, and my mentor asked me a simple question.

"Do you want to finally achieve all of your dreams, make a lot of money in the process, and do it without years in college or hoping you win the lottery?"

For the first time in a long time, I felt hope again. That quickly, I found myself very curious about a real opportunity.

Yes, that's right.

That's exactly what I said as I held the book, "Yes, that's right."

Shaking my head up and down, I looked back down at the book and started to read a message very similar to what you are reading right now.

As I was reading, the man tapped me on the shoulder and said, "Enjoy the book. Read it tonight, and I'll pick it back up from you tomorrow."

"Why are you letting me read this? I mean—."

As I was asking, he interrupted my question with a small laugh and walked away.

OK, I am curious. Wouldn't you be?

I opened up the book and began to read again.

Have you ever read a book that did more than just catch your attention, but it actually shifted the way you thought about something?

The book that I read, like this book, was one that reshaped my hopes and dreams again.

As I was finishing the book, I saw the name of the gentleman who gave me it to me scribbled with a simple message: "Ready for more? Call me."

Immediately, I picked up my phone, tapped out the number, and waited. The answer I got on his phone began with a question:

"If you could get paid, month after month, year after year for simply handing out this book to others, would you want to hear more?"

What?

I asked him to repeat that question.

"Sure", he replied. "If you could get paid month after month, even year after year for simply handing out this book to others, would you want to hear more about this system?"

I had never been asked anything like this before, and for just a moment, it sounded too good to be true. But he had caught my attention.

"So, I can get paid for handing out this book to others?" I asked.

"Yes. I get paid every single week for handing out this book and asking this same question to others," he told me.

"Tell me more."

Now, the story goes on until today with you reading this book and asking yourself if you would be willing to get paid for handing out books to others.

What is the magic behind handing out a book and getting paid?

It's called sifting.

Sifting

One of the best ways to understand "sifting" is to look at the daily work of a gold miner.

Now, I'm not talking about one who digs deep into caves and extracts huge boulders in an attempt to discover gold.

Instead, I'm talking about the one who sits on the edge of a river, ankle deep in the running water, sifting through rocks and debris "panning for gold."

The river will take all the rocks and sediment and wash it downstream to where the person will sift through all of the pebbles and dirt – until he sees a glimmer.

Gold is heavier than most minerals in a river causing it to go deeper and making it harder to discover. However, once you take a "gold pan" you can sift through all of the debris and as the water washes away all of the rocks – you have gold!

This book does exactly what the gold prospectors of the past did to find their fortune.

Like the prospector, it removes the debris and looks for the rocks that glitter and shine!

Yep, it sifts through many different people to find the ones who are as we like to call them, "Chosen."

If you are still reading this far into this book you can understand what "chosen" means:

- The 13-year-old kid who places advertisements in supermarket tabloids

- The stay-at-home mom who dreams about starting a home-based business

- The business executive who looks very professional on the outside, but is torn and twisted internally because he wants to find an escape hatch from the business grind

Maybe... you.

This book and the opportunity to get paid very well sharing it with others are not for everyone.

In fact, let's give you another chance right now to stop reading, close the cover, and laugh it off.

Here's your chance.

Still reading?

Even more curious than before?

You have just experienced "sifting."

You chose YOU.

Chosen.

Some people never made it this far in the book.

They listened to the voice of average and surrendered to mediocrity.

They were sifted and did not have the desire or courage to experience more in life.

Yet, here we are.

You are still reading. You have been sifted, open-minded, possibly even really hungry for more.

Let us continue...

My mentor taught me that there are only 2 types of people in the world, and knowing which kind you are is the first step to success.

The first types of people are close-minded to any form of opportunities outside of the ordinary occupation.

This does not make them "bad" people, but it does definitely limit their potential for growth and prosperity.

My old neighbor Steve was truly this type of person. He worked hard every day and did a good job of providing the basic needs for his family.

He worked 45 hours a week, took his normal 2 weeks of vacation each year, and planned on retiring at 65 hoping to still be healthy enough to do some fishing.

When anyone mentioned to Steve the possibility of another opportunity for wealth creation, even a great opportunity, Steve would miss out for fear of the unknown.

He valued "certainty" more than hope or opportunity.

This is how many people are today.

Average.

Safe.

Mediocre.

OK, let's be real!

If you are chosen, you will vividly see that "Steve" is absolutely boring!

And, most people in this area will just get by financially. Being broke is their harsh reality.

If you are chosen, you are not a "Steve" — and if you are a "Steve," that's OK — but this book is not for you.

The second type of people are open-minded and sometimes even actively searching for true opportunities to prosper financially, live out their dreams, and make goals a reality.

These types of people may be cautious, which is normal, but they never allow uncertainty to kill their dreams and desires.

My mentor was this type of person.

This type of person will read a book like this, pick up the phone, and call the person who handed him the book.

The second type of people never says, "I can't." Instead, they often ask themselves, "How can I?"

They have been called dreamers.

They have been told to be realistic, to calm down or even to "be happy for the jobs they have" as if the jobs were miracles endowed that could never be replaced.

The second type of person is still reading this book.

That person is chosen.

What about you?

Are you willing to risk the mundane everyday existence to once again experience hope and discover the power of opportunity?

This book is not to convince you, it is to simply sift and sort.

Are you the first type of person, a "Steve"?

It's perfectly OK if you are.

Or, are you the second type of person, like my mentor, and like the one who handed you this book?

Why Sifting and Sorting?

In the last decade, I have coached and consulted with people from all over the world when it comes to personal finance and building businesses that would pay them year after year.

I have learned what works and what doesn't.

I have discovered some secrets and short-cuts to true success. And I have seen people fail.

So, this book was born to help people just like you reach others without any objections or rejection.

We share this book with others in a similar way it was shared with you.

If people are open-minded to hearing more about a true business system that generates wealth, they give us back the book with a simple, "Tell me more."

However, if they are more like "Steve," and close-minded, they give us back the book with a simple, "no thanks."

That's it!

That's how simple it is to create a business that can pay you over and over for years to come!

We sort through the "Steves" using the book and only talk with people like us who are open-minded to hearing more.

We only talk with people who desire to have their hope restored and make their dreams a reality!

Hope.

Opportunity.

And, a proven system involving this simple book.

This system has created many multi-millionaires and has helped thousands retire sooner, make more money, and have fun again in their daily lives.

Are you chosen?

Are you open to the possibility of this book being the beginning of something amazing just like it was in my life?

Would you object to taking a look at a proven system to create wealth in your life?

And no, it does not include running ads in supermarket tabloids *(but, that sure was fun)*.

If you're open-minded, then get out your phone right now, yep, now.

Text the person who gave you this book.

Their number is _____.

Text them the message: "Tell me more."

That's it.

It gets really fun from that point.

If you are not open-minded and still reading (must be a great book, huh?) then text them and say, "No thanks."

It's OK either way.

Sifting and sorting.

That's as hard as it gets.

You can do that, yes?

If you can hand out this lil' book a few times a week, help those who say yes and thank the ones who say no, then you can have a lot of fun and earn a small fortune in the next few months.

What do you do when someone says, "Yes, tell me more"?

That is easy.

We introduce the person just like we would love to introduce you to a proven business opportunity and the fail-proof system that is generating substantial income for so many people today.

However, first, we are simply sorting and sifting.

Open-minded goal-oriented people say YES – and we build a fun business together.

Close-minded people say "No Thank You" – and we smile and move on.

Rejection-free.

Pain-free.

We get to build a Real Business with Real Money and have a lot of fun doing it!

Ready?

Let's get the ball rolling.

Let's chat further.

We look forward to hearing from you.

God bless,

Wayne Sutton

(910) 233-2511

Book Orders: To order more of these powerful books please contact us at 910-233-2511.

Get The Edge Systems

Post Office Box 1466

Carolina Beach NC 28428

www.ingramcontent.com/pod-product-compliance
Lightning Source LLC
Chambersburg PA
CBHW051335220526
45468CB00004B/1649